30 Minutes Cookbook

Simple and Satisfying Meal Ideas

Quick and Convenient Recipes for Busy Schedules

Suzy Anderson

Tables of the Contents

Breakfasts 7

Scrambled Eggs with Cheese and Herb 7

Peanut Butter and Banana Toast 8

Ham and Cheese Omelet 8

Yogurt Parfait with Fruit and Granola 9

English Muffin Breakfast Sandwich 10

Sweet Potato and Egg Breakfast Skillet 11

Peanut Butter Banana Toast 12

Veggie and Feta Scramble 12

Berry Yogurt Parfait 13

Ham and Egg Breakfast Burrito 14

Avocado Toast with Fried Egg 15

Blueberry Pancakes 16

Veggie Omelette 17

Quick and Easy Blueberry Muffins 18

Tomato and Basil Pasta 19

Ham and Cheese Omelette 20

Peanut Butter and Jelly French Toast 22

Avocado Toast with Egg 23

Greek Yogurt Berry Parfait 24

Banana Pancakes 25

Peanut Butter Banana Smoothie 26

Vegetable Mains 27

Roasted Vegetable Quinoa Bowl 27

Spicy Chickpea and Vegetable Stir-Fry 28

Zucchini Noodle Stir-Fry 29

Spinach and Feta Stuffed Bell Peppers 30

Roasted Vegetable Quinoa Bowl II 31

Grilled Vegetable and Halloumi Skewers 32

Creamy Tomato and Vegetable Pasta 33

Veggie and Chickpea Stir-Fry 34

Grilled Eggplant and Zucchini Salad 35

Broccoli and Cheddar Soup 36

Garlic Roasted Carrots 37

Chickpea and Spinach Stir-Fry 38

One-Pan Eggplant Parmesan 39

Spicy Peanut Noodles with Vegetables 41

Roasted Vegetable Quinoa Bowl III 42

Grilled Vegetable Skewers 43

Spicy Roasted Cauliflower 44

Grilled Zucchini and Carrot Noodles 45

Quick and Easy Veggie Stir Fry 46

Black Bean and Sweet Potato Tacos 47

Beans, Grains, and Pastas Recipes 49

Spicy Chickpea and Tomato Pasta 49

White Bean and Spinach Salad Ingredients: 50

Smoky Black Bean and Sweet Potato Skillet 50

Quick and Easy Bean and Rice Bowls 51

Spicy Three Bean Chili 52

White Bean and Pesto Pasta Salad 53

Creamy White Bean and Spinach Soup 54

Chickpea and Tomato Curry 55

Quick Quinoa and Vegetable Stir-Fry 56

Lemon and Herb Rice Bowl 57

Spicy Spanish Rice Bowl 58

Cheesy Broccoli and Brown Rice Casserole 59

Quick and Easy Tomato Basil Pasta 60

Creamy Avocado Pasta 61

Shrimp Scampi Pasta 62

Pesto Pasta with Roasted Cherry Tomatoes 64

Spicy Sausage and Bell Pepper Pasta 65

Shrimp Scampi Pasta 66

Creamy Tomato and Basil Pasta 68

Pesto Pasta with Cherry Tomatoes and Mozzarella 69

Fish & Seafood Recipes 70

Pan-Seared Salmon with Lemon and Thyme 70

Grilled Tilapia with Mango Salsa 71

Shrimp Scampi with Linguine 72

Mussels in White Wine and Garlic Sauce 73

Pan-Fried Tilapia with Lemon Butter Sauce 74

Spicy Shrimp Scampi 75

Lemon Garlic Shrimp Pasta 76

Pan-Seared Scallops with Angel Hair Pasta 78

Lemon Garlic Shrimp Scampi Pasta 79

Poultry and Meats Recipes 81

Pan-Fried Chicken Breasts with Lemon Butter Sauce 81

Quick and Easy Beef Stir-Fry 82

Quick and Easy Chicken Stir-Fry 83

Grilled Steak with Chimichurri Sauce 84

Quick Chicken Piccata 85

Sautéed Pork Chops 87

Spicy Chicken Stir-Fry 88

Garlic Butter Steak 89

Sautéed Chicken with Garlic and Lemon 90

Quick and Easy Pork Chops 91

Sautéed Chicken with Lemon and Garlic 92

Quick Chicken and Broccoli Stir-Fry 93

Pan-Seared Pork Chops with Honey-Mustard Glaze 94

Quick Chicken Stir Fry 95

Quick Beef and Broccoli 96

Quick and Easy Chicken Fajitas 97

Desserts Recipes 98

Quick Berry Sorbet 98

Microwave Nutella Mug Cake 99

Microwave Peanut Butter Mug Cake 100

Quick and Easy Fruit Sorbet 101

Quick and Easy Fruit Salad 102

Quick Berry Parfait 103

Chocolate Peanut Butter Mug Cake 104

Quick Berry Compote 105

Chocolate Peanut Butter Banana Bites 106

Quick and Easy Fruit Salad 107

Quick and Easy Berry Tart 107

Chocolate Peanut Butter Banana Muffins 108

Breakfasts

Scrambled Eggs with Cheese and Herb

Ingredients:

- 2 large eggs
- 1 tablespoon milk
- Salt and pepper to taste
- 1 tablespoon butter
- 1/4 cup shredded cheddar cheese
- 1 teaspoon chopped fresh chives or parsley

Instructions:

1. In a medium bowl, beat the eggs with milk, salt, and pepper.
2. In a non-stick pan, melt the butter over medium heat.
3. Pour in the beaten eggs and stir continuously until they are just set but still moist.
4. Remove the pan from heat and stir in the shredded cheese and chopped herbs until the cheese is melted.
5. Serve hot.

Peanut Butter and Banana Toast

Ingredients:

- 2 slices of whole grain bread
- 2 tablespoons peanut butter
- 1 ripe banana, sliced
- Honey to taste
- Cinnamon to taste

Instructions:

1. Toast the bread slices.
2. Spread the peanut butter over the toast.
3. Arrange the banana slices on top of the peanut butter.
4. Drizzle with honey and sprinkle with cinnamon.
5. Serve immediately.

Ham and Cheese Omelet

Ingredients:

- 2 large eggs
- Salt and pepper to taste
- 1 tablespoon milk
- 1 tablespoon butter

- 2 ounces deli ham, chopped
- 1/4 cup shredded cheddar cheese

Instructions:

1. In a medium bowl, whisk together the eggs, salt, pepper, and milk.
2. In a non-stick pan, heat the butter over medium heat.
3. Pour in the egg mixture and let it cook for 1-2 minutes, until set on the bottom.
4. Sprinkle the ham and cheese over one half of the omelet.
5. Use a spatula to fold the other half of the omelet over the filling.
6. Cook for an additional 1-2 minutes, until the cheese is melted and the eggs are fully cooked.
7. Serve hot.

Yogurt Parfait with Fruit and Granola

Ingredients:

- 1 cup Greek yogurt
- 1/2 cup mixed berries
- 1/4 cup granola
- Honey to taste

Instructions:

1. In a clear glass or bowl, layer the Greek yogurt, mixed berries, and granola.
2. Repeat the layers until all the ingredients are used.
3. Drizzle with honey and serve immediately.

English Muffin Breakfast Sandwich

Ingredients:

- 2 English muffins, split and toasted
- 2 eggs
- Salt and pepper to taste
- 2 slices of bacon, cooked
- 2 slices of cheese (cheddar, American, or Swiss)
- Butter or mayonnaise for spreading

Instructions:

1. In a non-stick pan, scramble the eggs with salt and pepper over medium heat until set.
2. Toast the English muffins and spread butter or mayonnaise on the inside.
3. Assemble the sandwich by layering the cheese, eggs, bacon, and the other half of the English muffin.
4. Serve hot.

Sweet Potato and Egg Breakfast Skillet

Ingredients:

- 1 medium sweet potato, peeled and diced
- 1 tablespoon olive oil
- Salt and pepper to taste
- 1 red bell pepper, diced
- 1/4 onion, diced
- 4 large eggs
- 1/4 cup shredded cheddar cheese
- Fresh herbs for garnish (optional)

Instructions:

1. In a large non-stick pan, heat the olive oil over medium heat.
2. Add the diced sweet potato and cook for 5-7 minutes, until tender.
3. Season with salt and pepper and add the diced red bell pepper and onion.
4. Cook for an additional 2-3 minutes, until the vegetables are softened.
5. In a small bowl, beat the eggs with salt and pepper.
6. Pour the beaten eggs over the vegetables in the pan and scramble until set.
7. Sprinkle the shredded cheese on top of the eggs and cook until melted.
8. Serve hot, garnished with fresh herbs if desired.

Peanut Butter Banana Toast

Ingredients:

- 2 slices of bread, toasted
- 2 tablespoons peanut butter
- 1 ripe banana, sliced
- Honey to taste
- Cinnamon to taste

Instructions:

1. Toast the bread and spread peanut butter on each slice.
2. Layer the sliced banana on top of the peanut butter.
3. Drizzle with honey and sprinkle with cinnamon.
4. Serve immediately.

Veggie and Feta Scramble

Ingredients:

- 4 large eggs
- Salt and pepper to taste
- 1 tablespoon milk
- 1 tablespoon olive oil
- 1/4 red onion, diced
- 1/2 bell pepper, diced
- 1 cup baby spinach

- 1/4 cup crumbled feta cheese
- Fresh herbs for garnish (optional)

Instructions:

1. In a medium bowl, whisk together the eggs, salt, pepper, and milk.
2. In a large non-stick pan, heat the olive oil over medium heat.
3. Add the diced onion and bell pepper and cook for 2-3 minutes, until softened.
4. Add the baby spinach and cook until wilted.
5. Pour the egg mixture over the vegetables in the pan and scramble until set.
6. Sprinkle the crumbled feta cheese on top of the eggs and cook until melted.
7. Serve hot, garnished with fresh herbs if desired.

Berry Yogurt Parfait

Ingredients:

- 1 cup plain Greek yogurt
- 1/4 cup mixed berries (strawberries, blueberries, raspberries)
- 2 tablespoons honey
- 1/4 cup granola

Instructions:

1. In a glass or bowl, layer the Greek yogurt, mixed berries, and granola.
2. Repeat the layering until all ingredients are used.
3. Drizzle with honey on top.
4. Serve immediately.

Ham and Egg Breakfast Burrito

Ingredients:

- 2 large flour tortillas
- 4 large eggs
- Salt and pepper to taste
- 1/4 cup diced ham
- 1/4 cup shredded cheddar cheese
- Salsa or hot sauce for serving (optional)

Instructions:

1. In a medium bowl, whisk together the eggs, salt, pepper, and diced ham.
2. In a large non-stick pan, cook the egg mixture over medium heat, stirring occasionally, until set.
3. Warm the flour tortillas in the microwave or on a griddle.

4. Spoon the cooked egg mixture onto the center of each tortilla.
5. Sprinkle with shredded cheese.
6. Roll up the tortilla tightly to form a burrito.
7. Serve hot with salsa or hot sauce, if desired.

Avocado Toast with Fried Egg

Ingredients:

- 2 slices of bread, toasted
- 1 ripe avocado, pitted and mashed
- Salt and pepper to taste
- 2 large eggs
- Olive oil for frying
- Fresh herbs for garnish (optional)

Instructions:

1. Toast the bread and spread the mashed avocado on each slice.
2. Sprinkle with salt and pepper.
3. In a non-stick pan, heat a small amount of olive oil over medium heat.

4. Crack the eggs into the pan and cook until the whites are set and the yolks are still runny, about 2-3 minutes.
5. Place the fried eggs on top of the avocado toast.
6. Serve hot, garnished with fresh herbs if desired.

Blueberry Pancakes

Ingredients:

- 1 cup all-purpose flour
- 2 teaspoons baking powder
- 1/4 teaspoon salt
- 1 large egg
- 1 cup milk
- 2 tablespoons unsalted butter, melted
- 1/2 cup fresh blueberries
- Maple syrup for serving

Instructions:

1. In a medium bowl, whisk together the flour, baking powder, and salt.
2. In a separate bowl, whisk together the egg, milk, and melted butter.
3. Add the wet ingredients to the dry ingredients and stir until just combined.
4. Gently fold in the blueberries.

5. In a non-stick pan or griddle over medium heat, scoop 1/4 cup of batter per pancake.
6. Cook until small bubbles form on the surface of the pancakes, then flip and cook until golden brown on both sides, about 2-3 minutes per side.
7. Serve hot with maple syrup.

Veggie Omelette

Ingredients:

- 4 large eggs
- Salt and pepper to taste
- 1/4 cup diced onion
- 1/4 cup diced bell pepper
- 1/4 cup diced mushrooms
- 1/4 cup shredded cheese
- 1 tablespoon olive oil

Instructions:

- In a medium bowl, whisk together the eggs, salt, and pepper.
- In a non-stick pan, heat the olive oil over medium heat.
- Add the onion, bell pepper, and mushrooms and cook until tender, about 5 minutes.
- Pour the egg mixture into the pan over the vegetables.

- As the eggs start to set, use a spatula to lift the edges of the omelette and let the uncooked egg run underneath.
- When the eggs are nearly set, sprinkle the shredded cheese over half of the omelette.
- Fold the other half of the omelette over the cheese.
- Cook until the cheese is melted, about 2-3 minutes.
- Serve hot.

Quick and Easy Blueberry Muffins

Ingredients:

- 2 cups all-purpose flour
- 2 teaspoons baking powder
- 1/2 teaspoon salt
- 1/2 cup white sugar
- 1 egg
- 1/2 cup milk
- 1/2 cup vegetable oil
- 1 teaspoon vanilla extract
- 1 cup fresh blueberries

Instructions:

1. Preheat the oven to 400°F (200°C). Line a muffin tin with paper liners or grease with cooking spray.

2. In a large mixing bowl, whisk together the flour, baking powder, salt, and sugar.
3. In another bowl, whisk together the egg, milk, oil, and vanilla extract.
4. Add the wet ingredients to the dry ingredients and mix until just combined.
5. Gently fold in the blueberries.
6. Fill each muffin cup about 2/3 of the way full with the batter.
7. Bake for 20-25 minutes, or until a toothpick inserted into the center of a muffin comes out clean.
8. Allow to cool for 5 minutes before serving.

Tomato and Basil Pasta

Ingredients:

- 1 lb. pasta
- 1 pint cherry tomatoes, halved
- 1/4 cup olive oil
- 4 cloves of garlic, minced
- 1/2 teaspoon salt
- 1/4 teaspoon black pepper
- 1/2 cup fresh basil, chopped
- 1/2 cup grated Parmesan cheese

Instructions:

1. Cook pasta according to package instructions until al dente. Reserve 1 cup of the pasta water.
2. While the pasta is cooking, heat the olive oil in a large skillet over medium heat.
3. Add the garlic, salt, and pepper and cook for 2 minutes, stirring constantly.
4. Add the cherry tomatoes and cook for 5-7 minutes, until they start to soften.
5. Drain the pasta and add it to the skillet with the tomato mixture.
6. Toss the pasta with the tomato mixture and add a splash of the reserved pasta water if needed to help the sauce coat the pasta.
7. Stir in the basil and Parmesan cheese.
8. Serve hot and enjoy!

Ham and Cheese Omelette

Ingredients:

- 3 large eggs
- 2 tablespoons milk
- Salt and pepper, to taste

- 1 tablespoon butter
- 1/2 cup diced ham
- 1/2 cup shredded cheddar cheese
- 2 tablespoons chopped fresh parsley (optional)

Instructions:

1. In a large mixing bowl, whisk together the eggs, milk, salt, and pepper.
2. Heat the butter in a non-stick skillet over medium heat.
3. Add the diced ham to the skillet and cook for 2-3 minutes, until slightly browned.
4. Pour the egg mixture into the skillet with the ham. Use a spatula to gently scramble the eggs.
5. Once the eggs are partially set, sprinkle the cheese on one half of the omelette.
6. Use the spatula to fold the other half of the omelette over the cheese.
7. Cook for another 2-3 minutes, until the cheese is melted and the eggs are fully set.
8. Serve the omelette hot, sprinkled with chopped parsley, if desired.

Peanut Butter and Jelly French Toast

Ingredients:

- 4 slices of bread
- 2 large eggs
- 1/2 cup milk
- 1/2 teaspoon vanilla extract
- Salt, to taste
- 2 tablespoons peanut butter
- 2 tablespoons jelly or jam
- Butter, for frying
- Powdered sugar, for serving (optional)

Instructions:

1. In a large mixing bowl, whisk together the eggs, milk, vanilla extract, and salt.
2. Spread the peanut butter on one slice of bread and the jelly on another slice.
3. Put the slices of bread together to form a sandwich.
4. Dip the sandwich into the egg mixture, making sure it is well coated on both sides.
5. Heat a non-stick skillet or griddle over medium heat and add a pat of butter.
6. Cook the sandwich in the skillet for 3-4 minutes on each side, until golden brown.
7. Repeat with the remaining sandwiches.
8. Serve the French toast hot, sprinkled with powdered sugar, if desired.

Avocado Toast with Egg

Ingredients:

- 2 slices of bread
- 1 ripe avocado
- 1 large egg
- Salt and pepper, to taste
- Butter, for frying
- Red pepper flakes, for serving (optional)

Instructions:

1. Toast the bread slices until golden brown.
2. In a small bowl, mash the avocado with a fork.
3. Spread the mashed avocado onto each slice of toast.
4. Heat a non-stick skillet over medium heat and add a pat of butter.
5. Crack the egg into the skillet and cook until the whites are set and the yolk is cooked to your liking.
6. Place the fried egg on top of one of the avocado-toasted slices.
7. Season with salt and pepper to taste.
8. Serve hot, sprinkled with red pepper flakes, if desired.

Greek Yogurt Berry Parfait

Ingredients:

- 1 cup Greek yogurt
- 1/4 cup granola
- 1/2 cup mixed berries (such as strawberries, blueberries, and raspberries)
- 1 tablespoon honey
- Fresh mint leaves, for serving (optional)

Instructions:

1. In a tall glass or bowl, layer half of the Greek yogurt at the bottom.
2. Top the yogurt with half of the granola.
3. Add another layer of the Greek yogurt, followed by the mixed berries.
4. Drizzle the honey over the berries.
5. Repeat the layers with the remaining Greek yogurt, granola, and mixed berries.
6. Serve chilled, topped with fresh mint leaves, if desired.

Banana Pancakes

Ingredients:

- 1 cup all-purpose flour
- 2 teaspoons baking powder
- 1/4 teaspoon salt
- 1 large egg
- 1 cup milk
- 1 ripe banana, mashed
- 1 tablespoon butter
- Maple syrup, for serving

Instructions:

1. In a large mixing bowl, whisk together the flour, baking powder, and salt.
2. In a separate bowl, whisk together the egg, milk, and mashed banana.
3. Pour the wet ingredients into the dry ingredients and whisk until just combined.
4. Heat a non-stick skillet over medium heat and add a pat of butter.
5. Using a 1/4 cup measuring cup, pour the batter onto the skillet, making 2-3 pancakes at a time.
6. Cook the pancakes for 2-3 minutes on each side, until bubbles form on the surface and the edges start to look set.
7. Repeat with the remaining batter.
8. Serve the pancakes hot with maple syrup.

Peanut Butter Banana Smoothie

Ingredients:

- 1 ripe banana
- 1 cup milk
- 1/2 cup Greek yogurt
- 2 tablespoons peanut butter
- 1 tablespoon honey
- 1 teaspoon vanilla extract
- 4 ice cubes

Instructions:

1. In a blender, combine the banana, milk, Greek yogurt, peanut butter, honey, and vanilla extract.
2. Add the ice cubes and blend until smooth.
3. Pour the smoothie into a glass and serve immediately.

Vegetable Mains

Roasted Vegetable Quinoa Bowl

Ingredients:

- 1 cup quinoa
- 2 cups mixed vegetables (such as bell peppers, zucchini, and cherry tomatoes)
- 2 tablespoons olive oil
- Salt and pepper, to taste
- 1/4 cup crumbled feta cheese
- Fresh basil leaves, for serving (optional)

Instructions:

1. Preheat the oven to 400°F.
2. Rinse the quinoa and cook according to package instructions.
3. Meanwhile, chop the mixed vegetables into bite-sized pieces.
4. On a large baking sheet, toss the chopped vegetables with olive oil, salt, and pepper.
5. Roast in the oven for 15-20 minutes, or until tender and lightly browned.
6. In a large bowl, combine the cooked quinoa with the roasted vegetables.

7. Sprinkle with crumbled feta cheese.
8. Serve hot or cold, garnished with fresh basil leaves, if desired.

Spicy Chickpea and Vegetable Stir-Fry

Ingredients:

- 1 can chickpeas, drained and rinsed
- 2 cups mixed vegetables (such as broccoli, carrots, and snap peas)
- 2 tablespoons vegetable oil
- 1 tablespoon minced ginger
- 2 cloves garlic, minced
- 1 tablespoon soy sauce
- 1 teaspoon chili paste
- Salt and pepper, to taste
- Fresh cilantro leaves, for serving (optional)

Instructions:

1. Wash and chop the mixed vegetables into bite-sized pieces.
2. In a large skillet or wok, heat the vegetable oil over high heat.
3. Add the ginger and garlic and stir-fry for 30 seconds.

4. Add the chickpeas and mixed vegetables and stir-fry for 3-5 minutes, or until the vegetables are tender.
5. Stir in the soy sauce, chili paste, salt, and pepper.
6. Serve hot, garnished with fresh cilantro leaves, if desired.

Zucchini Noodle Stir-Fry

Ingredients:

- 4 medium zucchini, spiralized
- 1 tablespoon vegetable oil
- 1 red bell pepper, sliced
- 1 cup sliced mushrooms
- 1 cup snap peas
- 2 cloves garlic, minced
- 2 tablespoons soy sauce
- 1 teaspoon honey
- Salt and pepper, to taste
- Fresh basil leaves, for serving (optional)

Instructions:

1. Spiralize the zucchini and set aside.
2. In a large skillet or wok, heat the vegetable oil over high heat.

3. Add the bell pepper, mushrooms, snap peas, and garlic and stir-fry for 3-5 minutes, or until the vegetables are tender.
4. Stir in the zucchini noodles, soy sauce, honey, salt, and pepper.
5. Stir-fry for 2-3 minutes, or until the zucchini noodles are heated through.
6. Serve hot, garnished with fresh basil leaves, if desired.

Spinach and Feta Stuffed Bell Peppers

Ingredients:

- 4 large bell peppers
- 1 tablespoon olive oil
- 1 onion, diced
- 1 cup cooked quinoa
- 1 (10 oz) package frozen chopped spinach, thawed and squeezed dry
- 1/2 cup crumbled feta cheese
- Salt and pepper, to taste
- Fresh parsley leaves, for serving (optional)

Instructions:

1. Preheat the oven to 400°F.

2. Cut the tops off of the bell peppers and remove the seeds.
3. In a large skillet, heat the olive oil over medium heat.
4. Add the onion and cook for 3-5 minutes, or until softened.
5. Stir in the cooked quinoa, chopped spinach, crumbled feta cheese, salt, and pepper.
6. Stuff the bell peppers with the quinoa mixture.
7. Place the stuffed bell peppers in a baking dish and bake for 20-25 minutes, or until the bell peppers are tender and the filling is heated through.
8. Serve hot, garnished with fresh parsley leaves, if desired.

Roasted Vegetable Quinoa Bowl II

Ingredients:

- 1 large sweet potato, peeled and diced
- 1 red bell pepper, sliced
- 1 yellow squash, diced
- 1 zucchini, diced
- 1 red onion, sliced
- 2 tablespoons olive oil
- Salt and pepper, to taste
- 1 cup quinoa, cooked
- Fresh parsley leaves, for serving (optional)

Instructions:

1. Preheat the oven to 400°F.
2. In a large bowl, combine the sweet potato, bell pepper, yellow squash, zucchini, red onion, olive oil, salt, and pepper.
3. Spread the vegetables out in a single layer on a baking sheet.
4. Roast the vegetables for 15-20 minutes, or until tender and golden.
5. Serve the roasted vegetables over cooked quinoa and garnish with fresh parsley leaves, if desired.

Grilled Vegetable and Halloumi Skewers

Ingredients:

- 1 red bell pepper, sliced
- 1 yellow squash, diced
- 1 zucchini, diced
- 1 red onion, sliced
- 8 oz halloumi cheese, cut into 1-inch pieces
- 2 tablespoons olive oil
- Salt and pepper, to taste
- Fresh mint leaves, for serving (optional)

Instructions:

1. Soak 8 wooden skewers in water for at least 30 minutes.
2. In a large bowl, combine the bell pepper, yellow squash, zucchini, red onion, halloumi cheese, olive oil, salt, and pepper.
3. Thread the vegetables and halloumi cheese onto the skewers, alternating between each.
4. Heat a grill or grill pan over medium heat.
5. Place the skewers on the grill and cook for 6-8 minutes, or until the vegetables are tender and the halloumi cheese is golden brown and crispy.
6. Serve hot, garnished with fresh mint leaves, if desired.

Creamy Tomato and Vegetable Pasta

Ingredients:

- 8 oz spaghetti
- 1 tablespoon olive oil
- 1 small onion, diced
- 2 cloves garlic, minced
- 1 red bell pepper, sliced
- 1 zucchini, diced
- 1 cup cherry tomatoes, halved
- 1/2 cup heavy cream
- Salt and pepper, to taste
- Fresh basil leaves, for serving (optional)

Instructions:

1. Cook the spaghetti according to package instructions, until al dente. Reserve 1 cup of pasta water.
2. In a large saucepan, heat the olive oil over medium heat. Add the onion and garlic and cook until soft and fragrant, about 2-3 minutes.
3. Add the bell pepper, zucchini, cherry tomatoes, heavy cream, salt, and pepper. Cook, stirring occasionally, until the vegetables are tender and the sauce has thickened, about 10 minutes.
4. Drain the spaghetti and add it to the saucepan, tossing to coat the pasta with the sauce. If the sauce is too thick, add a little of the reserved pasta water.
5. Serve hot, garnished with fresh basil leaves, if desired.

Veggie and Chickpea Stir-Fry

Ingredients:

- 1 tablespoon olive oil
- 1 small onion, diced
- 2 cloves garlic, minced
- 1 red bell pepper, sliced
- 1 zucchini, diced
- 1 cup cherry tomatoes, halved
- 1 can chickpeas, drained and rinsed

- Salt and pepper, to taste
- Fresh cilantro leaves, for serving (optional)

Instructions:

1. In a large wok or frying pan, heat the olive oil over medium heat. Add the onion and garlic and cook until soft and fragrant, about 2-3 minutes.
2. Add the bell pepper, zucchini, cherry tomatoes, chickpeas, salt, and pepper. Cook, stirring occasionally, until the vegetables are tender and the chickpeas are hot, about 8-10 minutes.
3. Serve hot, garnished with fresh cilantro leaves, if desired.

Grilled Eggplant and Zucchini Salad

Ingredients:

- 2 medium eggplants, sliced into rounds
- 2 medium zucchinis, sliced into rounds
- 1/4 cup olive oil
- Salt and pepper, to taste
- 1/2 lemon, juiced
- 2 tablespoons balsamic vinegar
- 1/4 cup crumbled feta cheese
- Fresh basil leaves, for serving (optional)

Instructions:

1. Preheat a grill or grill pan to medium-high heat.
2. Brush the eggplant and zucchini rounds with the olive oil and season with salt and pepper.
3. Place the eggplant and zucchini on the grill and cook until tender and slightly charred, about 5-7 minutes per side.
4. In a small bowl, whisk together the lemon juice, balsamic vinegar, and a pinch of salt and pepper.
5. In a large bowl, arrange the grilled eggplant and zucchini rounds and drizzle with the lemon-balsamic dressing.
6. Sprinkle with crumbled feta cheese and garnish with fresh basil leaves, if desired. Serve warm.

Broccoli and Cheddar Soup

Ingredients:

- 1 tablespoon olive oil
- 1 small onion, diced
- 2 cloves garlic, minced
- 4 cups broccoli florets
- 4 cups vegetable broth
- 1/2 cup heavy cream
- Salt and pepper, to taste

- 1 cup grated cheddar cheese
- Fresh parsley leaves, for serving (optional)

Instructions:

1. In a large saucepan, heat the olive oil over medium heat. Add the onion and garlic and cook until soft and fragrant, about 2-3 minutes.
2. Add the broccoli, vegetable broth, heavy cream, salt, and pepper. Bring to a boil, then reduce the heat and simmer until the broccoli is tender, about 8-10 minutes.
3. Using an immersion blender or transferring the mixture to a blender or food processor, puree the soup until smooth.
4. Return the soup to the saucepan and heat until hot. Stir in the grated cheddar cheese until melted.
5. Serve hot, garnished with fresh parsley leaves, if desired.

Garlic Roasted Carrots

Ingredients:

- 1 pound carrots, peeled and cut into thin rounds
- 4 cloves garlic, minced
- 2 tablespoons olive oil
- Salt and pepper, to taste
- 1 teaspoon dried thyme

- 1 lemon, zested and juiced
- 2 tablespoons chopped parsley

Instructions:

1. Preheat the oven to 400°F (200°C). Line a baking sheet with parchment paper.
2. In a large bowl, combine the carrots, garlic, olive oil, salt, pepper, and thyme. Toss to coat.
3. Arrange the carrots on the prepared baking sheet in a single layer. Roast in the oven until tender and slightly browned, about 15-20 minutes.
4. In a small bowl, whisk together the lemon zest, lemon juice, and parsley.
5. Serve the roasted carrots hot, drizzled with the lemon-parsley dressing.

Chickpea and Spinach Stir-Fry

Ingredients:

- 1 tablespoon olive oil
- 1 small onion, diced
- 2 cloves garlic, minced
- 1 can chickpeas, drained and rinsed
- 2 cups baby spinach
- Salt and pepper, to taste

- Juice of 1/2 lemon
- 1/4 cup crumbled feta cheese

Instructions:

1. In a large skillet, heat the olive oil over medium heat. Add the onion and garlic and cook until soft and fragrant, about 2-3 minutes.
2. Add the chickpeas and cook until slightly browned, about 5 minutes.
3. Stir in the baby spinach and cook until wilted, about 2-3 minutes.
4. Season with salt, pepper, and lemon juice.
5. Serve the chickpea and spinach stir-fry hot, topped with crumbled feta cheese.

One-Pan Eggplant Parmesan

Ingredients:

- 1 medium eggplant, sliced into rounds
- 1 cup panko breadcrumbs
- 1/2 cup grated parmesan cheese
- 1 teaspoon dried basil
- 1 teaspoon dried oregano
- Salt and pepper, to taste
- 2 eggs, beaten

- 1/2 cup all-purpose flour
- 1 cup marinara sauce
- 1 cup shredded mozzarella cheese
- Fresh basil leaves, for garnish

Instructions:

1. Preheat the oven to 400°F (200°C). Line a baking sheet with parchment paper.
2. In a shallow dish, combine the panko breadcrumbs, parmesan cheese, dried basil, dried oregano, salt, and pepper.
3. In another shallow dish, beat the eggs.
4. Place the flour in a third shallow dish.
5. Dip each eggplant slice first in the flour, then in the beaten eggs, and finally in the breadcrumb mixture.
6. Place the breaded eggplant slices on the prepared baking sheet.
7. Bake in the oven for 15 minutes.
8. Remove from the oven and spread the marinara sauce over the eggplant slices. Sprinkle with mozzarella cheese.
9. Return to the oven and bake until the cheese is melted and bubbly, about 10 minutes.
10. Serve hot, garnished with fresh basil leaves.

Spicy Peanut Noodles with Vegetables

Ingredients:

- 8 ounces linguine or spaghetti
- 2 tablespoons olive oil
- 1 red bell pepper, sliced
- 1 yellow onion, sliced
- 2 cloves garlic, minced
- 1 tablespoon grated ginger
- 1 tablespoon chili paste
- 1/2 cup creamy peanut butter
- 1/2 cup low-sodium vegetable broth
- 1/4 cup soy sauce
- 2 tablespoons rice vinegar
- 1 tablespoon honey
- Salt and pepper, to taste
- 1 cup snow peas
- 2 carrots, julienned
- 1/4 cup chopped peanuts, for garnish
- Fresh cilantro leaves, for garnish

Instructions:

1. Cook the pasta according to package instructions until al dente. Reserve 1/2 cup of the pasta water.
2. In a large skillet, heat the olive oil over medium heat. Add the red bell pepper, onion, garlic, and ginger and cook until soft and fragrant, about 5 minutes.
3. Stir in the chili paste and cook for 1 minute.

4. In a small bowl, whisk together the peanut butter, vegetable broth, soy sauce, rice vinegar, honey, salt, and pepper.
5. Stir the peanut sauce into the skillet with the vegetables.
6. Add the snow peas, carrots, and reserved pasta water to the skillet and bring to a simmer. Cook until the vegetables are tender and the sauce has thickened, about 5 minutes.
7. Toss the sauce with the cooked pasta.
8. Serve hot, garnished with chopped peanuts and cilantro leaves.

Roasted Vegetable Quinoa Bowl III

Ingredients:

- 1 cup of quinoa
- 2 large carrots, chopped
- 1 large red bell pepper, chopped
- 1 large yellow onion, chopped
- 1 large zucchini, chopped
- 4 cloves of garlic, minced
- 2 tablespoons of olive oil
- 1 teaspoon of dried basil
- 1 teaspoon of dried thyme
- Salt and pepper to taste

Instructions:

1. Preheat the oven to 400°F (204°C).
2. In a large bowl, mix together the chopped carrots, bell pepper, onion, zucchini, and minced garlic.
3. Drizzle the olive oil over the vegetables and add the dried basil, dried thyme, salt, and pepper. Toss until everything is well coated.
4. Spread the mixture out evenly on a baking sheet and roast for 20 minutes or until the vegetables are tender and slightly browned.
5. While the vegetables are roasting, cook the quinoa according to the package instructions.
6. Serve the roasted vegetables over a bed of cooked quinoa.

Grilled Vegetable Skewers

Ingredients:

- 1 large eggplant, sliced into 1-inch rounds
- 2 red bell peppers, sliced into 1-inch pieces
- 2 yellow onions, sliced into wedges
- 8-10 mushrooms, stems removed
- 2 tablespoons of olive oil
- 1 teaspoon of dried oregano

- 1 teaspoon of dried basil
- Salt and pepper to taste
- 8-10 wooden skewers, soaked in water for 30 minutes

Instructions:

1. Preheat the grill to medium-high heat.
2. In a large bowl, mix together the sliced eggplant, bell peppers, onion, and mushrooms.
3. Drizzle the olive oil over the vegetables and add the dried oregano, dried basil, salt, and pepper. Toss until everything is well coated.
4. Skewer the vegetables, alternating between different types.
5. Grill the vegetable skewers for 10-12 minutes, turning occasionally, until they are slightly charred and tender.
6. Serve the grilled vegetable skewers with your favorite dipping sauce.

Spicy Roasted Cauliflower

Ingredients:

- 1 large head of cauliflower, chopped into florets
- 2 tbsp olive oil
- 1 tsp chili powder
- 1 tsp paprika

- 1 tsp garlic powder
- Salt and pepper, to taste
- 1 lemon, sliced

Instructions:

1. Preheat the oven to 425°F (220°C).
2. In a large bowl, combine the cauliflower florets, olive oil, chili powder, paprika, garlic powder, salt, and pepper. Toss to coat the cauliflower evenly.
3. Spread the coated cauliflower in a single layer on a baking sheet and bake for 20-25 minutes, or until tender and golden brown, flipping once during cooking.
4. Squeeze the lemon slices over the roasted cauliflower and serve hot.

Grilled Zucchini and Carrot Noodles

Ingredients:

- 2 medium zucchinis, spiralized or julienned
- 2 large carrots, spiralized or julienned
- 1 tbsp olive oil
- 1 tsp dried basil
- 1 tsp dried oregano
- Salt and pepper, to taste

Instructions:

1. Heat a grill pan over medium-high heat.
2. In a large bowl, combine the zucchini noodles, carrot noodles, olive oil, basil, oregano, salt, and pepper. Toss to evenly coat the vegetables.
3. Grill the vegetables, stirring occasionally, for 5-7 minutes, or until slightly charred and tender.
4. Serve the grilled zucchini and carrot noodles hot as a side dish or add some grilled chicken or tofu for a complete meal.

Quick and Easy Veggie Stir Fry

Ingredients:

- 1 tablespoon oil
- 1 red pepper, sliced
- 1 yellow onion, sliced
- 1 cup sliced mushrooms
- 1 cup sliced carrots
- 2 cloves garlic, minced
- 1 tablespoon soy sauce
- 1 tablespoon cornstarch
- 2 cups cooked rice

Instructions:

1. Heat oil in a large wok or skillet over high heat.
2. Add the red pepper, onion, mushrooms, carrots, and garlic and stir-fry for 2-3 minutes or until the vegetables are tender.
3. In a small bowl, whisk together the soy sauce and cornstarch.
4. Pour the mixture over the vegetables and stir until the sauce has thickened.
5. Serve the stir-fry over cooked rice.

Black Bean and Sweet Potato Tacos

Ingredients:

- 1 large sweet potato, peeled and diced
- 1 tablespoon oil
- 1 can black beans, rinsed and drained
- 1 teaspoon chili powder
- 1/2 teaspoon cumin
- Salt and pepper, to taste
- 8 corn tortillas
- 1 avocado, diced
- 1/2 cup shredded cheese
- 1/2 cup salsa

Instructions:

1. Preheat the oven to 400°F.
2. Toss the sweet potato with oil and spread on a baking sheet. Bake for 20 minutes, or until tender.
3. In a medium saucepan, heat the black beans with chili powder, cumin, salt, and pepper over medium heat until heated through.
4. Warm the tortillas in the oven or in a dry pan.
5. To assemble the tacos, place some sweet potato, black beans, avocado, cheese, and salsa on each tortilla.

Beans, Grains, and Pastas Recipes

Spicy Chickpea and Tomato Pasta

Ingredients:

- 1 pound spaghetti
- 1 can chickpeas, drained and rinsed
- 2 tablespoons olive oil
- 3 cloves garlic, minced
- 1 can diced tomatoes
- 1 teaspoon red pepper flakes
- Salt and pepper, to taste
- Fresh basil, chopped
- Grated Parmesan cheese (optional)

Instructions:

1. Cook spaghetti according to package instructions until al dente. Drain and set aside.
2. In a large skillet, heat the olive oil over medium heat.
3. Add the garlic and cook for 30 seconds, or until fragrant.
4. Add the chickpeas, diced tomatoes, red pepper flakes, salt, and pepper. Simmer for 5-7 minutes, or until heated through.
5. Toss the spaghetti with the chickpea mixture and garnish with fresh basil and Parmesan cheese, if desired.

White Bean and Spinach Salad Ingredients:

- 1 can white beans, drained and rinsed
- 1 cup cherry tomatoes, halved
- 2 cups baby spinach
- 1/4 cup red onion, diced
- 2 tablespoons balsamic vinegar
- 1 tablespoon olive oil
- Salt and pepper, to taste

Instructions:

1. In a large bowl, combine the white beans, cherry tomatoes, baby spinach, and red onion.
2. In a small bowl, whisk together the balsamic vinegar, olive oil, salt, and pepper.
3. Pour the dressing over the salad and toss to combine. Serve immediately.

Smoky Black Bean and Sweet Potato Skillet

Ingredients:

- 1 large sweet potato, peeled and diced
- 1 tablespoon oil
- 1 can black beans, drained and rinsed

- 1 teaspoon smoked paprika
- 1/2 teaspoon cumin
- Salt and pepper, to taste
- 1/4 cup chopped fresh cilantro
- Fresh lime wedges (optional)

Instructions:

1. In a large skillet, heat the oil over medium heat.
2. Add the sweet potato and cook for 7-8 minutes, or until tender.
3. Add the black beans, smoked paprika, cumin, salt, and pepper to the skillet and cook for 2-3 minutes, or until heated through.
4. Stir in the cilantro and serve with lime wedges, if desired.

Quick and Easy Bean and Rice Bowls

Ingredients:

- 1 cup long grain white rice
- 1 can black beans, drained and rinsed
- 1 can corn kernels, drained
- 1/4 cup salsa
- 1 avocado, diced
- Fresh cilantro, chopped
- Fresh lime wedges (optional)

Instructions:

1. Cook the rice according to package instructions.
2. In a medium saucepan, heat the black beans, corn, and salsa over medium heat until heated through.
3. To assemble the bowls, divide the rice among four serving bowls and top with the bean mixture, avocado, cilantro, and a squeeze of fresh lime juice, if desired.

Spicy Three Bean Chili

Ingredients:

- 1 tablespoon oil
- 1 medium onion, diced
- 2 cloves garlic, minced
- 1 can black beans, drained and rinsed
- 1 can kidney beans, drained and rinsed
- 1 can diced tomatoes
- 2 teaspoons chili powder
- 1 teaspoon cumin
- Salt and pepper, to taste
- Grated cheddar cheese (optional)
- Chopped green onions (optional)

Instructions:

1. In a large saucepan, heat the oil over medium heat.
2. Add the onion and cook until softened, about 5 minutes.
3. Add the garlic and cook for 30 seconds, or until fragrant.
4. Add the black beans, kidney beans, diced tomatoes, chili powder, cumin, salt, and pepper to the pan. Simmer for 10-15 minutes, or until heated through.
5. Serve with grated cheddar cheese and chopped green onions, if desired.

White Bean and Pesto Pasta Salad

Ingredients:

- 1 pound rotini pasta
- 1 can white beans, drained and rinsed
- 1 cup cherry tomatoes, halved
- 1/2 cup pesto
- Salt and pepper, to taste
- Fresh basil, chopped
- Grated Parmesan cheese (optional)

Instructions:

1. Cook the pasta according to package instructions until al dente. Drain and rinse with cold water.
2. In a large bowl, combine the cooked pasta, white beans, cherry tomatoes, pesto, salt, and pepper.

3. Toss until evenly coated.
4. Garnish with fresh basil and Parmesan cheese, if desired.

Creamy White Bean and Spinach Soup

Ingredients:

- 1 tablespoon oil
- 1 medium onion, diced
- 2 cloves garlic, minced
- 4 cups vegetable broth
- 1 can white beans, drained and rinsed
- 2 cups fresh spinach
- Salt and pepper, to taste
- 1/2 cup heavy cream
- Freshly grated Parmesan cheese (optional)

Instructions:

1. In a large saucepan, heat the oil over medium heat.
2. Add the onion and cook until softened, about 5 minutes.
3. Add the garlic and cook for 30 seconds, or until fragrant.
4. Add the vegetable broth and white beans to the pan. Bring to a boil and then reduce heat to low.
5. Using an immersion blender or a regular blender, puree the soup until smooth.

6. Add the spinach to the soup and cook until wilted, about 2 minutes.
7. Stir in the heavy cream, salt, and pepper.
8. Serve with grated Parmesan cheese, if desired.

Chickpea and Tomato Curry

Ingredients:

- 1 tablespoon oil
- 1 medium onion, diced
- 2 cloves garlic, minced
- 1 can chickpeas, drained and rinsed
- 1 can diced tomatoes
- 1 tablespoon curry powder
- Salt and pepper, to taste
- Cooked rice, for serving
- Fresh cilantro, chopped (optional)

Instructions:

1. In a large saucepan, heat the oil over medium heat.
2. Add the onion and cook until softened, about 5 minutes.
3. Add the garlic and cook for 30 seconds, or until fragrant.
4. Add the chickpeas, diced tomatoes, curry powder, salt, and pepper to the pan. Simmer for 10-15 minutes, or until heated through.

5. Serve over cooked rice and garnish with cilantro, if desired.

Quick Quinoa and Vegetable Stir-Fry

Ingredients:

- 1 tablespoon oil
- 1 medium onion, diced
- 2 cloves garlic, minced
- 2 cups cooked quinoa
- 2 cups mixed vegetables (such as bell peppers, carrots, and snow peas)
- 2 tablespoons soy sauce
- 1 teaspoon ginger, grated
- Salt and pepper, to taste
- Sesame seeds (optional)
- Fresh cilantro, chopped (optional)

Instructions:

1. In a large wok or frying pan, heat the oil over high heat.
2. Add the onion and cook until softened, about 5 minutes.
3. Add the garlic and cook for 30 seconds, or until fragrant.
4. Add the cooked quinoa and mixed vegetables to the pan and stir-fry until the vegetables are tender, about 5-7 minutes.
5. Stir in the soy sauce, ginger, salt, and pepper.

6. Serve topped with sesame seeds and fresh cilantro, if desired.

Lemon and Herb Rice Bowl

Ingredients:

- 1 cup long-grain white rice
- 2 cups water
- 1 lemon, juiced
- 1 tablespoon dried herbs (such as thyme and basil)
- Salt and pepper, to taste
- Grilled chicken, for serving (optional)
- Fresh parsley, chopped (optional)

Instructions:

1. In a medium saucepan, combine the rice, water, lemon juice, herbs, salt, and pepper. Bring to a boil.
2. Reduce heat to low, cover, and simmer until the rice is tender and the liquid has been absorbed, about 18-20 minutes.
3. Serve with grilled chicken, if desired, and topped with fresh parsley.

Spicy Spanish Rice Bowl

Ingredients:

- 1 tablespoon oil
- 1 medium onion, diced
- 1 green bell pepper, diced
- 2 cloves garlic, minced
- 1 cup long-grain white rice
- 2 cups vegetable broth
- 1 teaspoon paprika
- 1/2 teaspoon cumin
- Salt and pepper, to taste
- 1 can of diced tomatoes with green chilies
- Fresh cilantro, chopped (optional)

Instructions:

1. In a large saucepan, heat the oil over medium heat.
2. Add the onion and green pepper and cook until softened, about 5 minutes.
3. Add the garlic and cook for 30 seconds, or until fragrant.
4. Stir in the rice, broth, paprika, cumin, salt, and pepper. Bring to a boil.
5. Reduce heat to low, cover, and simmer until the rice is tender and the liquid has been absorbed, about 18-20 minutes.
6. Stir in the diced tomatoes with green chilies.

7. Serve topped with fresh cilantro, if desired.

Cheesy Broccoli and Brown Rice Casserole

Ingredients:

- 1 cup brown rice
- 2 cups water
- 2 cups broccoli florets
- 1 cup shredded cheddar cheese
- 1/2 cup milk
- 1 tablespoon butter
- 2 tablespoons all-purpose flour
- Salt and pepper, to taste

Instructions:

1. Preheat oven to 375°F.
2. In a medium saucepan, combine the rice and water. Bring to a boil.
3. Reduce heat to low, cover, and simmer until the rice is tender and the liquid has been absorbed, about 18-20 minutes.
4. In a separate saucepan, steam the broccoli until tender, about 5 minutes.
5. In a saucepan over medium heat, melt the butter. Whisk in the flour and cook for 1 minute.

6. Gradually add the milk, whisking continuously until the mixture thickens, about 2-3 minutes.
7. Stir in the cheese until melted and smooth.
8. In a large casserole dish, combine the cooked rice, steamed broccoli, and cheese sauce.
9. Bake in the preheated oven for 15 minutes, or until the top is golden brown. Serve hot.

Quick and Easy Tomato Basil Pasta

Ingredients:

- 1 pound of penne pasta
- 2 tablespoons of olive oil
- 4 cloves of garlic, minced
- 1 can of diced tomatoes (14.5 oz)
- 1 teaspoon of dried basil
- Salt and pepper to taste
- 1/2 cup of grated parmesan cheese
- Fresh basil leaves for garnish

Instructions:

1. Cook pasta according to package instructions until al dente. Reserve 1 cup of pasta water.

2. In a large skillet, heat the olive oil over medium heat. Add minced garlic and cook until fragrant, about 1 minute.
3. Add the diced tomatoes, dried basil, salt, and pepper to the skillet. Stir to combine and bring the sauce to a simmer.
4. Drain the pasta and add it to the sauce. Toss the pasta in the sauce until well combined. If the sauce is too thick, add a little bit of the reserved pasta water to reach the desired consistency.
5. Serve the pasta in bowls and sprinkle with grated parmesan cheese. Garnish with fresh basil leaves.

Creamy Avocado Pasta

Ingredients:

- 1 pound of spaghetti pasta
- 2 ripe avocados
- 1/2 cup of heavy cream
- 2 cloves of garlic, minced
- 1/2 teaspoon of red pepper flakes
- Salt and pepper to taste
- 1/2 cup of grated parmesan cheese
- Fresh cilantro leaves for garnish

Instructions:

1. Cook pasta according to package instructions until al dente. Reserve 1 cup of pasta water.
2. In a blender, puree the avocados, heavy cream, minced garlic, red pepper flakes, salt, and pepper until smooth.
3. In a large skillet, heat the avocado sauce over medium heat. Stir in a little bit of the reserved pasta water to reach the desired consistency.
4. Drain the pasta and add it to the sauce. Toss the pasta in the sauce until well combined.
5. Serve the pasta in bowls and sprinkle with grated parmesan cheese. Garnish with fresh cilantro leaves.

Shrimp Scampi Pasta

Ingredients:

- 1 pound of linguine pasta
- 1 lb of large shrimp, peeled and deveined
- 4 tablespoons of unsalted butter
- 4 cloves of garlic, minced
- 1/2 cup of white wine
- 1/2 lemon, juiced
- Salt and pepper to taste
- 1/4 cup of chopped fresh parsley

- Grated parmesan cheese for serving

Instructions:

1. Cook pasta according to package instructions until al dente. Reserve 1 cup of pasta water.
2. In a large skillet, melt the butter over medium heat. Add the minced garlic and cook until fragrant, about 1 minute.
3. Add the shrimp to the skillet and cook until pink and cooked through, about 2-3 minutes per side. Remove the shrimp from the skillet and set aside.
4. Add the white wine and lemon juice to the skillet and bring to a simmer. Cook for 2-3 minutes or until the sauce has reduced by half. Season with salt and pepper to taste.
5. Drain the pasta and add it to the sauce. Toss the pasta in the sauce until well combined. If the sauce is too thick, add a little bit of the reserved pasta water to reach the desired consistency.
6. Return the shrimp to the skillet and toss until well combined. Serve the pasta in bowls and sprinkle with chopped parsley and grated parmesan cheese.

Pesto Pasta with Roasted Cherry Tomatoes

Ingredients:

- 1 pound of fusilli pasta
- 2 cups of cherry tomatoes, halved
- 2 tablespoons of olive oil
- Salt and pepper to taste
- 1/2 cup of prepared basil pesto
- 1/4 cup of toasted pine nuts
- Grated parmesan cheese for serving

Instructions:

1. Preheat oven to 400°F. Line a baking sheet with parchment paper.
2. On the prepared baking sheet, toss the cherry tomatoes with olive oil, salt, and pepper. Roast in the oven for 20-25 minutes or until the tomatoes are soft and slightly charred.
3. Cook pasta according to package instructions until al dente. Reserve 1 cup of pasta water.
4. In a large bowl, mix the cooked pasta with the prepared pesto until well combined. If the pasta is too dry, add a little bit of the reserved pasta water to reach the desired consistency.

5. Add the roasted cherry tomatoes and toasted pine nuts to the pasta and mix until well combined. Serve in bowls and sprinkle with grated parmesan cheese.

Spicy Sausage and Bell Pepper Pasta

Ingredients:

- 1 pound of linguine pasta
- 1 tablespoon of olive oil
- 1 pound of Italian sausage, casing removed
- 2 bell peppers, sliced
- 4 cloves of garlic, minced
- Red pepper flakes to taste
- Salt and pepper to taste
- 1/2 cup of chicken broth
- Grated parmesan cheese for serving

Instructions:

1. Cook pasta according to package instructions until al dente. Reserve 1 cup of pasta water.
2. In a large skillet, heat the olive oil over medium heat. Add the sausage and cook, breaking it up into small pieces, until browned and crispy, about 5-7 minutes.

3. Add the sliced bell peppers to the skillet and cook until tender, about 5 minutes. Add the minced garlic and red pepper flakes, and cook until fragrant, about 1 minute.
4. Season with salt and pepper to taste. Pour in the chicken broth and bring to a boil. Reduce heat and let the sauce simmer for 2-3 minutes.
5. Drain the pasta and add it to the skillet. Toss the pasta in the sauce until well combined. If the sauce is too thick, add a little bit of the reserved pasta water to reach the desired consistency.
6. Serve the pasta in bowls and sprinkle with grated parmesan cheese.

Shrimp Scampi Pasta

Ingredients:

- 1 pound of spaghetti pasta
- 2 tablespoons of butter
- 4 cloves of garlic, minced
- 1 pound of raw shrimp, peeled and deveined
- Salt and pepper to taste
- 1/4 cup of white wine
- 1 lemon, juiced
- 1/2 cup of chopped fresh parsley
- Grated parmesan cheese for serving

Instructions:

1. Cook pasta according to package instructions until al dente. Reserve 1 cup of pasta water.
2. In a large skillet, melt the butter over medium heat. Add the minced garlic and cook until fragrant, about 1 minute.
3. Add the shrimp to the skillet and cook until pink and slightly charred, about 3-5 minutes. Season with salt and pepper to taste.
4. Pour in the white wine and lemon juice, and let the sauce simmer for 2-3 minutes. Stir in the chopped parsley and mix until well combined.
5. Drain the pasta and add it to the skillet. Toss the pasta in the sauce until well combined. If the pasta is too dry, add a little bit of the reserved pasta water to reach the desired consistency.
6. Serve the pasta in bowls and sprinkle with grated parmesan cheese.

Creamy Tomato and Basil Pasta

Ingredients:

- 1 pound of fettuccine pasta
- 2 tablespoons of olive oil
- 4 cloves of garlic, minced
- 1 can of crushed tomatoes (14 ounces)
- Salt and pepper to taste
- 1/2 cup of heavy cream
- 1/2 cup of chopped fresh basil
- Grated parmesan cheese for serving

Instructions:

1. Cook pasta according to package instructions until al dente. Reserve 1 cup of pasta water.
2. In a large skillet, heat the olive oil over medium heat. Add the minced garlic and cook until fragrant, about 1 minute.
3. Pour in the crushed tomatoes and season with salt and pepper to taste. Let the sauce simmer for 2-3 minutes.
4. Pour in the heavy cream and stir in the chopped basil. Let the sauce simmer for 2-3 minutes.
5. Drain the pasta and add it to the skillet. Toss the pasta in the sauce until well combined. If the sauce is too thick, add a little bit of the reserved pasta water to reach the desired consistency.
6. Serve the pasta in bowls and sprinkle with grated parmesan cheese.

Pesto Pasta with Cherry Tomatoes and Mozzarella

Ingredients:

- 1 pound of penne pasta
- 2 tablespoons of olive oil
- 1 cup of prepared basil pesto
- 1 pint of cherry tomatoes, halved
- 8 ounces of mozzarella cheese, cubed
- Salt and pepper to taste
- Grated parmesan cheese for serving

Instructions:

1. Cook pasta according to package instructions until al dente. Reserve 1 cup of pasta water.
2. In a large skillet, heat the olive oil over medium heat. Pour in the prepared pesto and let it warm up for 1-2 minutes.
3. Add the halved cherry tomatoes and cubed mozzarella cheese to the skillet. Season with salt and pepper to taste. Let the sauce simmer for 2-3 minutes, until the cheese has melted and the tomatoes are tender.
4. Drain the pasta and add it to the skillet. Toss the pasta in the sauce until well combined. If the pasta is too dry, add a little bit of the reserved pasta water to reach the desired consistency.
5. Serve the pasta in bowls and sprinkle with grated parmesan cheese.

Fish & Seafood Recipes

Pan-Seared Salmon with Lemon and Thyme

Ingredients:

- 4 salmon fillets, skin-on
- Salt and pepper to taste
- 2 tablespoons of olive oil
- 4 cloves of garlic, minced
- 4 sprigs of fresh thyme
- 2 lemons, sliced
- Fresh thyme leaves for serving

Instructions:

1. Season the salmon fillets with salt and pepper on both sides.
2. In a large skillet, heat the olive oil over medium-high heat. Place the salmon fillets in the skillet, skin-side down. Cook the salmon for 4-5 minutes, until the skin is crispy and golden brown.
3. Flip the salmon fillets over and add the minced garlic, thyme sprigs, and lemon slices to the skillet. Cook the salmon for 2-3 minutes, until the flesh is cooked through and the lemon slices are tender.
4. Serve the salmon on a serving platter, topped with the crispy garlic and thyme, and the tender lemon slices. Garnish with fresh thyme leaves.

Grilled Tilapia with Mango Salsa

Ingredients:

- 4 tilapia fillets
- Salt and pepper to taste
- 2 tablespoons of olive oil
- 1 ripe mango, peeled and diced
- 1 red bell pepper, diced
- 1/2 red onion, diced
- 1/4 cup of chopped fresh cilantro
- Juice of 1 lime
- Fresh cilantro leaves for serving

Instructions:

1. Season the tilapia fillets with salt and pepper on both sides.
2. In a bowl, mix together the diced mango, red bell pepper, red onion, chopped cilantro, and lime juice. Season the mango salsa with salt and pepper to taste.
3. Heat a grill or a grill pan over medium-high heat. Brush the tilapia fillets with olive oil and grill for 4-5 minutes on each side, until the flesh is cooked through and the grill marks are visible.
4. Serve the grilled tilapia on a serving platter, topped with the fresh mango salsa. Garnish with fresh cilantro leaves.

Shrimp Scampi with Linguine

Ingredients:

- 8 ounces of linguine
-
- Salt and pepper to taste
- 2 tablespoons of olive oil
- 4 cloves of garlic, minced
- 1 pound of large shrimp, peeled and deveined
- 1/4 cup of white wine
- 2 tablespoons of butter
- Juice of 1 lemon
- Fresh parsley leaves for serving

Instructions:

1. Cook the linguine according to package instructions, in a pot of boiling salted water, until al dente. Reserve 1 cup of pasta cooking water.
2. In a large skillet, heat the olive oil over medium-high heat. Add the minced garlic and cook until fragrant, about 1 minute. Add the shrimp to the skillet and season with salt and pepper to taste. Cook the shrimp for 2-3 minutes, until they turn pink and are cooked through.
3. Add the white wine to the skillet and let it cook for 1-2 minutes, until it reduces by half. Add the butter and lemon juice to the skillet and stir to combine.
4. Drain the cooked linguine and add it to the skillet with the shrimp scampi sauce. Toss the linguine with the

sauce until evenly coated. If the sauce is too thick, add some of the reserved pasta cooking water to thin it out.

5. Serve the shrimp scampi linguine on a serving platter, garnished with fresh parsley leaves.

Mussels in White Wine and Garlic Sauce

Ingredients:

- 2 pounds of mussels, scrubbed and debearded
- Salt and pepper to taste
- 2 tablespoons of olive oil
- 4 cloves of garlic, minced
- 1/2 cup of white wine
- 2 tablespoons of butter
- Juice of 1 lemon
- Fresh parsley leaves for serving

Instructions:

1. In a large saucepan, heat the olive oil over medium-high heat. Add the minced garlic and cook until fragrant, about 1 minute.
2. Add the mussels to the saucepan and season with salt and pepper to taste. Pour the white wine over the mussels and cover the saucepan with a lid. Cook the

mussels for 5-7 minutes, until they open up. Discard any mussels that do not open.

3. Add the butter and lemon juice to the saucepan and stir to combine. Cook the mussels in the sauce for 2-3 minutes, until the sauce is thick and creamy.
4. Serve the mussels in the white wine and garlic sauce on a serving platter, garnished with fresh parsley leaves.

Pan-Fried Tilapia with Lemon Butter Sauce

Ingredients:

- 4 Tilapia fillets
- 1 cup all-purpose flour
- 1 teaspoon paprika
- 1 teaspoon garlic powder
- Salt and pepper to taste
- 2 tablespoons olive oil
- 4 tablespoons butter
- 2 tablespoons lemon juice
- 1 teaspoon lemon zest
- 2 tablespoons fresh parsley, chopped

Instructions:

1. In a shallow dish, mix together the flour, paprika, garlic powder, salt, and pepper.

2. Dip the tilapia fillets in the mixture to coat.
3. Heat the olive oil in a large skillet over medium heat.
4. Add the coated fillets to the skillet and cook for 3-4 minutes on each side or until golden brown.
5. Remove the fillets from the skillet and keep warm.
6. In the same skillet, add the butter and melt it over medium heat.
7. Add the lemon juice and zest, stirring to combine.
8. Spoon the sauce over the cooked tilapia fillets.
9. Sprinkle with fresh parsley and serve with your favorite sides.

Spicy Shrimp Scampi

Ingredients:

- 1 pound raw shrimp, peeled and deveined
- 3 cloves garlic, minced
- 1 teaspoon red pepper flakes
- 1 teaspoon dried basil
- Salt and pepper to taste
- 2 tablespoons olive oil
- 1 lemon, juiced
- 2 tablespoons unsalted butter
- 2 tablespoons fresh parsley, chopped
- 1 tablespoon grated parmesan cheese

Instructions:

1. In a bowl, mix together the garlic, red pepper flakes, dried basil, salt, and pepper.
2. Add the shrimp to the bowl and toss to coat with the spice mixture.
3. Heat the olive oil in a large skillet over medium heat.
4. Add the shrimp to the skillet and cook for 2-3 minutes on each side or until pink and cooked through.
5. Remove the shrimp from the skillet and keep warm.
6. In the same skillet, add the lemon juice, butter, and parsley, stirring until the butter is melted.
7. Return the shrimp to the skillet and toss to coat with the sauce.
8. Sprinkle with parmesan cheese and serve immediately with your favorite pasta or rice.

Lemon Garlic Shrimp Pasta

Ingredients:

- 1 pound large shrimp, peeled and deveined
- 1/2 pound linguine pasta
- 3 tablespoons olive oil
- 4 cloves garlic, minced
- 1/4 teaspoon red pepper flakes
- Zest of 1 lemon

- Juice of 1 lemon
- Salt and black pepper, to taste
- 1/4 cup chopped fresh parsley

Instructions:

1. Cook the linguine pasta according to the package instructions. Reserve 1 cup of pasta water and drain the rest.
2. In a large pan, heat the olive oil over medium heat. Add the minced garlic and red pepper flakes and cook until fragrant, about 1 minute.
3. Add the shrimp to the pan and cook until pink and opaque, about 2-3 minutes. Season with salt and black pepper.
4. Add the lemon zest and juice to the pan and stir to combine.
5. Add the cooked linguine and parsley to the pan and toss to combine. If the pasta seems too dry, add a bit of the reserved pasta water.
6. Serve hot with additional lemon wedges and grated Parmesan cheese.

Pan-Seared Scallops with Angel Hair Pasta

Ingredients:

- 1 pound sea scallops
- 1/2 pound angel hair pasta
- 2 tablespoons butter
- 2 tablespoons olive oil
- 4 cloves garlic, minced
- Salt and black pepper, to taste
- 1/4 cup chopped fresh parsley
- Zest of 1 lemon

Instructions:

1. Cook the angel hair pasta according to the package instructions. Reserve 1 cup of pasta water and drain the rest.
2. In a large pan, heat the butter and olive oil over medium heat. Add the minced garlic and cook until fragrant, about 1 minute.
3. Pat the scallops dry with paper towels and season with salt and black pepper.
4. Add the scallops to the pan and cook until browned on both sides and just cooked through, about 2-3 minutes per side.
5. Add the cooked angel hair pasta and parsley to the pan and toss to combine. If the pasta seems too dry, add a bit of the reserved pasta water.
6. Serve hot with lemon zest and grated Parmesan cheese.

Lemon Garlic Shrimp Scampi Pasta

Ingredients:

- 1 pound of shrimp, peeled and deveined
- 1 pound of spaghetti pasta
- 1/4 cup of butter
- 4 cloves of garlic, minced
- 1 lemon, juiced
- 1/4 cup of white wine
- 1/4 teaspoon of red pepper flakes
- Salt and pepper to taste
- 1/4 cup of chopped parsley

Directions:

1. Cook the spaghetti pasta according to package instructions, until al dente. Reserve 1 cup of pasta water.
2. In a large skillet, heat the butter over medium heat. Add the garlic and cook until fragrant, about 1 minute.
3. Add the shrimp to the skillet and cook until pink, about 3-4 minutes.
4. Stir in the lemon juice, white wine, red pepper flakes, salt, and pepper. Cook until the sauce has thickened, about 2-3 minutes.
5. Drain the pasta and add it to the skillet. Toss until evenly coated with the sauce.
6. If the sauce is too thick, add some of the reserved pasta water to thin it out.

7. Serve the pasta with a sprinkle of chopped parsley and additional lemon wedges, if desired.

Poultry and Meats Recipes

Pan-Fried Chicken Breasts with Lemon Butter Sauce

Ingredients:

- 4 boneless, skinless chicken breasts
- Salt and pepper
- 2 tablespoons of all-purpose flour
- 2 tablespoons of olive oil
- 2 tablespoons of unsalted butter
- 2 cloves of garlic, minced
- 1 lemon, juiced
- 2 tablespoons of fresh parsley, chopped

Instructions:

1. Season the chicken breasts with salt and pepper.
2. Place the flour in a shallow dish, then coat each chicken breast in the flour, shaking off any excess.
3. Heat the olive oil in a large pan over medium heat.
4. Add the chicken breasts to the pan and cook for 5-6 minutes on each side, or until golden brown and cooked through.
5. Remove the chicken from the pan and place on a serving plate.
6. In the same pan, melt the butter over medium heat.

7. Add the garlic and cook for 1 minute, stirring constantly.
8. Stir in the lemon juice and parsley.
9. Pour the lemon butter sauce over the chicken breasts and serve.

Quick and Easy Beef Stir-Fry

Ingredients:

- 1 pound of sirloin steak, sliced into thin strips
- Salt and pepper
- 2 tablespoons of vegetable oil
- 1 red bell pepper, sliced
- 1 yellow onion, sliced
- 2 cloves of garlic, minced
- 1 cup of sliced mushrooms
- 2 tablespoons of soy sauce
- 1 tablespoon of cornstarch
- 1 tablespoon of water

Instructions:

1. Season the sliced steak with salt and pepper.
2. Heat the vegetable oil in a large wok or pan over high heat.
3. Add the steak to the pan and stir-fry for 2-3 minutes, or until browned.

4. Remove the steak from the pan and set aside.
5. Add the red bell pepper, onion, garlic, and mushrooms to the same pan and stir-fry for 3-4 minutes, or until tender.
6. Return the steak to the pan, then stir in the soy sauce.
7. In a small bowl, mix together the cornstarch and water.
8. Pour the cornstarch mixture into the pan and stir until the sauce thickens.
9. Serve the stir-fry over rice or noodles.

Quick and Easy Chicken Stir-Fry

Ingredients:

- 1 lb boneless, skinless chicken breasts, sliced into thin strips
- 2 tbsp soy sauce
- 2 tbsp cornstarch
- 1 tbsp vegetable oil
- 2 cloves garlic, minced
- 1 red bell pepper, sliced
- 1 green bell pepper, sliced
- 1 onion, sliced
- 2 tbsp hoisin sauce
- 2 tbsp water
- Salt and pepper to taste

Instructions:

1. In a large bowl, mix together the sliced chicken, soy sauce, and cornstarch.
2. Heat oil in a large wok or frying pan over high heat.
3. Add the garlic, red and green bell peppers, and onion to the pan. Cook until vegetables are slightly softened, about 2 minutes.
4. Add the chicken mixture to the pan and stir-fry until the chicken is no longer pink and vegetables are tender, about 5 minutes.
5. In a small bowl, whisk together the hoisin sauce and water.
6. Pour the hoisin sauce mixture into the pan and stir to coat the chicken and vegetables.
7. Serve the stir-fry over steamed rice or noodles. Season with salt and pepper to taste.

Grilled Steak with Chimichurri Sauce

Ingredients:

- 1 lb sirloin steak
- Salt and pepper to taste
- 1 clove garlic, minced
- 1/4 cup fresh parsley, chopped

- 1/4 cup fresh cilantro, chopped
- 2 tbsp red wine vinegar
- 1/4 cup olive oil
- Salt and pepper to taste

Instructions:

1. Season the steak with salt and pepper on both sides.
2. Heat a grill or grill pan to high heat.
3. Grill the steak for 4-5 minutes on each side for medium-rare, or to desired doneness.
4. Meanwhile, in a small bowl, mix together the garlic, parsley, cilantro, red wine vinegar, olive oil, salt, and pepper.
5. Serve the grilled steak with the chimichurri sauce on the side. Enjoy!

Quick Chicken Piccata

Ingredients:

- 4 boneless, skinless chicken breasts
- 1/2 cup all-purpose flour
- 1 teaspoon salt
- 1/2 teaspoon black pepper
- 2 tablespoons olive oil
- 1/2 cup chicken broth

- 1/2 cup lemon juice
- 1/4 cup capers
- 2 cloves garlic, minced
- 2 tablespoons unsalted butter
- 2 tablespoons chopped fresh parsley

Instructions:

1. In a shallow dish, mix together flour, salt, and pepper. Dredge the chicken in the flour mixture to coat.
2. In a large skillet, heat the olive oil over medium-high heat. Add the chicken and cook until browned, about 3-4 minutes per side.
3. Remove the chicken from the skillet and set aside.
4. Add the chicken broth, lemon juice, capers, and garlic to the skillet. Stir and bring to a boil.
5. Reduce the heat to low and return the chicken to the skillet. Cover and cook for 5 minutes, or until the chicken is fully cooked.
6. Remove the chicken from the skillet and set aside.
7. Add the butter to the sauce and whisk until melted. Pour the sauce over the chicken.
8. Sprinkle with chopped parsley and serve.

Sautéed Pork Chops

Ingredients:

- 4 bone-in pork chops
- Salt and pepper, to taste
- 1/4 cup all-purpose flour
- 2 tablespoons olive oil
- 1 medium onion, sliced
- 2 cloves garlic, minced
- 1 cup chicken broth
- 1/4 cup white wine
- 2 tablespoons fresh thyme leaves

Instructions:

1. Season the pork chops with salt and pepper. Dredge the chops in flour to coat.
2. In a large skillet, heat the olive oil over medium-high heat. Add the pork chops and cook until browned, about 3-4 minutes per side.
3. Remove the pork chops from the skillet and set aside.
4. Add the onion and garlic to the skillet. Sauté until softened, about 3-4 minutes.
5. Add the chicken broth, white wine, and thyme leaves to the skillet. Stir to combine.
6. Return the pork chops to the skillet and spoon the sauce over the chops.
7. Reduce the heat to low, cover the skillet, and simmer for 10-12 minutes, or until the pork chops are fully cooked.

8. Serve the pork chops with the sauce.

Spicy Chicken Stir-Fry

Ingredients:

- 1 lb boneless, skinless chicken breast, sliced into thin strips
- 1 red bell pepper, sliced
- 1 yellow onion, sliced
- 2 cloves garlic, minced
- 1 tablespoon ginger, grated
- 2 tablespoons soy sauce
- 2 tablespoons chili sauce
- 2 tablespoons cornstarch
- 2 tablespoons vegetable oil

Instructions:

1. In a small bowl, whisk together soy sauce, chili sauce, and cornstarch.
2. In a large wok or frying pan, heat the oil over high heat.
3. Add the chicken strips and stir-fry for 3-4 minutes until browned.
4. Add the red bell pepper, yellow onion, garlic, and ginger to the pan. Stir-fry for another 2-3 minutes.

5. Pour the sauce mixture over the stir-fry and continue to cook, stirring constantly, for another 2-3 minutes until the sauce thickens and the chicken is fully cooked.
6. Serve over rice or noodles.

Garlic Butter Steak

Ingredients:

- 2 (8 oz) sirloin steaks
- 2 tablespoons butter
- 4 cloves garlic, minced
- Salt and pepper, to taste

Instructions:

1. Preheat a large skillet over medium-high heat.
2. Season the steaks with salt and pepper.
3. Add the butter to the skillet and let it melt.
4. Add the steaks to the skillet and cook for 3-4 minutes per side, or until the desired level of doneness is reached.
5. During the last minute of cooking, add the minced garlic to the skillet and let it cook until fragrant.
6. Remove the steaks from the skillet and let them rest for a few minutes.
7. Serve with the garlic butter spooned on top.

Sautéed Chicken with Garlic and Lemon

Ingredients:

- 4 boneless chicken breasts
- Salt and pepper to taste
- 2 tablespoons olive oil
- 2 garlic cloves, minced
- 1 lemon, juiced
- 2 tablespoons butter
- Fresh parsley, chopped (optional)

Instructions:

1. Season chicken breasts with salt and pepper.
2. In a large pan, heat olive oil over medium heat.
3. Add chicken breasts and cook for 5-7 minutes on each side or until golden brown.
4. Add minced garlic to the pan and cook for an additional 30 seconds.
5. Remove the chicken from the pan and set aside.
6. In the same pan, add lemon juice and butter. Stir until the butter has melted.
7. Return chicken to the pan and coat with the lemon sauce.
8. Serve hot with chopped parsley on top (optional).

Quick and Easy Pork Chops

Ingredients:

- 4 pork chops
- Salt and pepper to taste
- 2 tablespoons olive oil
- 2 tablespoons Dijon mustard
- 2 tablespoons honey
- 2 tablespoons soy sauce

Instructions:

1. Season pork chops with salt and pepper.
2. In a large pan, heat olive oil over medium heat.
3. Add pork chops to the pan and cook for 4-5 minutes on each side or until fully cooked.
4. In a small bowl, mix together Dijon mustard, honey, and soy sauce.
5. Brush the mixture over the pork chops and cook for an additional 2-3 minutes, until the glaze has thickened.
6. Serve hot with your choice of sides.
7.

Sautéed Chicken with Lemon and Garlic

Ingredients:

- 4 boneless, skinless chicken breasts
- Salt and pepper to taste
- 3 tablespoons olive oil
- 4 cloves garlic, minced
- 1 lemon, juiced
- 2 tablespoons chopped fresh parsley

Instructions:

1. Season the chicken breasts with salt and pepper on both sides.
2. In a large skillet, heat the olive oil over medium-high heat.
3. Add the chicken breasts to the skillet and cook for 4-5 minutes on each side, or until golden brown and fully cooked through.
4. Remove the chicken from the skillet and set aside on a plate.
5. In the same skillet, add the minced garlic and cook for 30 seconds, or until fragrant.
6. Add the lemon juice to the skillet and stir to combine.
7. Return the chicken to the skillet and spoon the lemon and garlic mixture over the chicken.
8. Garnish with chopped parsley and serve immediately.

Quick Chicken and Broccoli Stir-Fry

Ingredients:

- 1 pound boneless, skinless chicken breasts, sliced into thin strips
- 2 cups broccoli florets
- 1 red bell pepper, sliced
- 2 cloves garlic, minced
- 2 tablespoons soy sauce
- 2 tablespoons hoisin sauce
- 1 tablespoon cornstarch
- 2 tablespoons vegetable oil

Instructions:

1. In a small bowl, whisk together soy sauce, hoisin sauce, and cornstarch.
2. In a large skillet, heat 1 tablespoon of oil over high heat. Add the chicken strips and cook until browned and cooked through, about 5 minutes. Remove the chicken from the skillet and set aside.
3. In the same skillet, add the remaining oil and stir in the broccoli, red bell pepper, and garlic. Cook until the vegetables are crisp-tender, about 3 minutes.
4. Return the chicken to the skillet and pour in the sauce. Cook, stirring, until the sauce has thickened, about 2 minutes. Serve hot over rice.

Pan-Seared Pork Chops with Honey-Mustard Glaze

Ingredients:

- 4 boneless pork chops
- Salt and pepper
- 1 tablespoon olive oil
- 2 tablespoons Dijon mustard
- 2 tablespoons honey
- 2 tablespoons apple cider vinegar
- 1 clove garlic, minced

Instructions:

1. Season both sides of the pork chops with salt and pepper.
2. In a large skillet, heat the olive oil over medium-high heat. Add the pork chops and cook until golden brown on both sides and cooked through, about 6 minutes per side.
3. In a small bowl, whisk together the mustard, honey, vinegar, and garlic.
4. Remove the pork chops from the skillet and place on a serving platter. Brush the honey-mustard glaze over the top of each pork chop. Serve hot.

Quick Chicken Stir Fry

Ingredients:

- 1 pound boneless, skinless chicken breasts, sliced into thin strips
- 2 tablespoons oil
- 1 red bell pepper, sliced
- 1 yellow onion, sliced
- 2 cloves garlic, minced
- 2 tablespoons soy sauce
- 1 tablespoon cornstarch
- 2 tablespoons water
- Salt and pepper to taste
- Rice or noodles to serve

Instructions:

1. In a large pan, heat oil over medium-high heat.
2. Add chicken and cook until browned, about 5 minutes.
3. Add the red bell pepper, yellow onion, and garlic to the pan and stir fry until they are soft and tender, about 5 minutes.
4. In a small bowl, whisk together the soy sauce, cornstarch, water, salt and pepper.
5. Pour the sauce over the chicken and vegetables and stir until everything is well coated.
6. Cook for an additional 2-3 minutes, or until the sauce thickens and the chicken is cooked through.
7. Serve hot with rice or noodles.

Quick Beef and Broccoli

Ingredients:

- 1 pound sirloin steak, sliced into thin strips
- 2 tablespoons oil
- 2 cups fresh broccoli florets
- 1 red onion, sliced
- 2 cloves garlic, minced
- 2 tablespoons soy sauce
- 1 tablespoon cornstarch
- 2 tablespoons water
- Salt and pepper to taste
- Rice to serve

Instructions:

1. In a large pan, heat oil over medium-high heat.
2. Add the steak and cook until browned, about 5 minutes.
3. Add the broccoli, red onion, and garlic to the pan and stir fry until they are soft and tender, about 5 minutes.
4. In a small bowl, whisk together the soy sauce, cornstarch, water, salt and pepper.
5. Pour the sauce over the steak and vegetables and stir until everything is well coated.
6. Cook for an additional 2-3 minutes, or until the sauce thickens and the steak is cooked through.
7. Serve hot with rice.

Quick and Easy Chicken Fajitas

Ingredients:

- 1 lb boneless, skinless chicken breasts, sliced into strips
- 2 bell peppers, sliced
- 1 onion, sliced
- 2 cloves garlic, minced
- 2 tbsp olive oil
- 1 tsp chili powder
- 1 tsp paprika
- 1 tsp cumin
- 1 tsp salt
- 1/2 tsp black pepper
- 8 flour tortillas
- Optional toppings: shredded cheese, sour cream, salsa, chopped cilantro

Instructions:

1. Heat a large skillet over medium-high heat.
2. Add the olive oil, chicken strips, bell peppers, onion, and garlic to the skillet.
3. Sprinkle the chili powder, paprika, cumin, salt, and black pepper over the chicken and vegetables.
4. Cook for 8-10 minutes, stirring occasionally, until the chicken is fully cooked and the vegetables are tender.
5. Serve the chicken and vegetables in warm flour tortillas with optional toppings as desired.

Desserts Recipes

Quick Berry Sorbet

Ingredients:

- 2 cups mixed berries (strawberries, blueberries, raspberries)
- 1/2 cup sugar
- 1/2 cup water
- 1 tbsp lemon juice

Instructions:

1. In a saucepan, heat the sugar and water over medium heat until the sugar dissolves.
2. Add the mixed berries and lemon juice to the saucepan and bring to a boil.
3. Reduce the heat and let the mixture simmer for 5 minutes or until the berries have broken down.
4. Remove from heat and let the mixture cool for 5 minutes.
5. Pour the mixture into a blender and blend until smooth.
6. Pour the mixture into a freezer-safe container and freeze for 2 hours.
7. Scoop the sorbet into serving dishes and serve immediately.

Microwave Nutella Mug Cake

Ingredients:

- 4 tbsp all-purpose flour
- 4 tbsp granulated sugar
- 2 tbsp unsweetened cocoa powder
- 2 tbsp Nutella
- 3 tbsp milk
- 1 egg
- 1/4 tsp baking powder

Instructions:

1. In a microwave-safe mug, mix together the flour, sugar, cocoa powder, Nutella, milk, egg, and baking powder until well combined.
2. Microwave the mixture on high for 2 minutes or until the cake has risen and is firm to the touch.
3. Serve the mug cake immediately, topped with a scoop of vanilla ice cream or whipped cream if desired.

Microwave Peanut Butter Mug Cake

Ingredients:

- 4 tablespoons all-purpose flour
- 4 tablespoons granulated sugar
- 2 tablespoons unsalted creamy peanut butter
- 2 tablespoons unsweetened cocoa powder
- 3 tablespoons milk
- 1 egg
- 1/4 teaspoon baking powder
- 1/8 teaspoon salt

Instructions:

1. In a microwave-safe mug, mix together the flour, sugar, peanut butter, cocoa powder, milk, egg, baking powder, and salt.
2. Stir the mixture until it is well combined and smooth.
3. Microwave the mug cake on high for 1 minute and 30 seconds, or until the cake has risen and is set.
4. Let the cake cool for a few minutes before serving, and enjoy!

Quick and Easy Fruit Sorbet

Ingredients:

- 4 cups of frozen mixed fruit
- 1/2 cup of granulated sugar
- 1/2 cup of water
- 2 tablespoons of lemon juice
- 1/4 teaspoon of salt

Instructions:

1. In a medium saucepan, heat the sugar, water, lemon juice, and salt over medium heat until the sugar has completely dissolved.
2. Remove the saucepan from the heat and let the mixture cool to room temperature.
3. In a blender or food processor, blend the frozen fruit until it is broken down into small pieces.
4. Gradually add the cooled sugar mixture to the blended fruit, blending until smooth.
5. Pour the mixture into a container and freeze for about 30 minutes, or until the sorbet is firm.
6. Serve the sorbet in bowls and enjoy!

Quick and Easy Fruit Salad

Ingredients:

- 2 cups mixed fresh fruit (e.g. strawberries, blueberries, grapes, melon, kiwi)
- 1/4 cup orange juice
- 1 tablespoon honey
- 1/2 teaspoon vanilla extract
- 1 tablespoon chopped mint (optional)

Instructions:

1. Wash and chop the mixed fruit and place them in a large bowl.
2. In a separate bowl, whisk together the orange juice, honey, and vanilla extract.
3. Pour the dressing over the fruit and mix well.
4. Sprinkle with the chopped mint, if using.
5. Serve chilled.

Quick Berry Parfait

Ingredients:

- 1 cup of mixed berries (strawberries, blueberries, raspberries)
- 1/2 cup of Greek yogurt
- 2 tbsp of honey
- 1/4 cup of granola

Instructions:

1. Wash the mixed berries and let them drain.
2. In a mixing bowl, combine the Greek yogurt and honey until fully incorporated.
3. Take a tall glass and layer the ingredients: first the yogurt mixture, then the mixed berries, and then the granola. Repeat the layers until all ingredients are used.
4. Serve the parfait chilled and enjoy!

Chocolate Peanut Butter Mug Cake

Ingredients:

- 4 tbsp of all-purpose flour
- 4 tbsp of sugar
- 2 tbsp of cocoa powder
- 2 tbsp of peanut butter
- 3 tbsp of milk
- 1 egg
- 1/4 tsp of baking powder
- a pinch of salt

Instructions:

1. In a large mug, mix together the flour, sugar, cocoa powder, baking powder, and salt.
2. Add the egg, peanut butter, and milk, and whisk until well combined.
3. Microwave the mug on high for 1 minute and 30 seconds or until the cake is cooked through.
4. Let the mug cake cool for a minute and then top with a drizzle of chocolate syrup or some melted chocolate.
5. Serve the mug cake warm and enjoy!

Quick Berry Compote

Ingredients:

- 2 cups mixed berries (strawberries, raspberries, blackberries, etc.)
- 1/4 cup sugar
- 2 tablespoons lemon juice
- 1 teaspoon cornstarch
- 1/4 teaspoon vanilla extract
- Pinch of salt

Instructions:

1. Rinse the berries and drain well.
2. In a medium saucepan, combine the sugar, lemon juice, cornstarch, vanilla extract, and salt. Stir until the sugar and cornstarch have dissolved.
3. Add the mixed berries to the saucepan and stir to combine.
4. Place the saucepan over medium heat and cook, stirring occasionally, until the mixture thickens and the berries have broken down, about 10-12 minutes.
5. Remove the compote from heat and let it cool slightly. Serve warm or at room temperature.

Chocolate Peanut Butter Banana Bites

Ingredients:

- 4 ripe bananas
- 1/4 cup peanut butter
- 1/4 cup melted chocolate
- Chopped peanuts (optional)

Instructions:

1. Peel and slice the bananas into rounds.
2. Spread peanut butter onto each banana slice.
3. Place the banana slices onto a sheet of wax paper and freeze for 10-15 minutes.
4. Dip each peanut butter-covered banana slice into the melted chocolate, using a toothpick to hold it.
5. Place the coated banana slices back onto the wax paper and sprinkle with chopped peanuts, if using.
6. Return the banana bites to the freezer until the chocolate has hardened, about 5-10 minutes. Serve immediately.

Quick and Easy Fruit Salad

Ingredients:

- 2 cups mixed fresh fruit (such as strawberries, blueberries, grapes, melon, etc.)
- 1 tbsp honey
- 1 tbsp lemon juice
- 1 tbsp chopped fresh mint

Instructions:

1. Wash and chop the mixed fruit into bite-sized pieces.
2. In a bowl, whisk together the honey, lemon juice, and mint.
3. Add the chopped fruit to the bowl and gently toss to combine.
4. Serve immediately or refrigerate until ready to eat.

Quick and Easy Berry Tart

Ingredients:

- 1 pre-made pie crust
- 1 cup mixed berries (strawberries, blueberries, raspberries)
- 1/4 cup granulated sugar

- 2 tablespoons cornstarch
- 1 tablespoon lemon juice
- 1 teaspoon vanilla extract
- 1/4 teaspoon salt

Instructions:

1. Preheat the oven to 375°F.
2. In a mixing bowl, combine the mixed berries, sugar, cornstarch, lemon juice, vanilla extract, and salt. Mix well.
3. Roll out the pie crust and place it in a 9-inch tart pan.
4. Pour the berry mixture into the crust.
5. Bake for 25-30 minutes or until the crust is golden brown and the filling is bubbly.
6. Let it cool completely and serve with a dollop of whipped cream.

Chocolate Peanut Butter Banana Muffins

Ingredients:

- 1 cup all-purpose flour
- 1 teaspoon baking powder
- 1/4 teaspoon baking soda
- 1/4 teaspoon salt
- 1/2 cup granulated sugar

- 1/2 cup creamy peanut butter
- 1 ripe banana, mashed
- 1 egg
- 1/2 cup milk
- 1/2 cup semi-sweet chocolate chips

Instructions:

1. Preheat the oven to 375°F.
2. In a large mixing bowl, whisk together the flour, baking powder, baking soda, and salt.
3. In a separate bowl, beat together the sugar, peanut butter, mashed banana, egg, and milk.
4. Add the wet ingredients to the dry ingredients and mix until just combined.
5. Fold in the chocolate chips.
6. Spoon the batter into a muffin tin lined with muffin cups, filling each about 2/3 of the way full.
7. Bake for 20-25 minutes or until a toothpick inserted into the center of a muffin comes out clean.
8. Let cool for 5 minutes in the muffin tin, then transfer to a wire rack to cool completely. Serve warm or at room temperature.

CPSIA information can be obtained
at www.ICGtesting.com
Printed in the USA
LVHW080550280223
740519LV00015B/291

9 788367 110594